ELCO 80-Foot PT Boat

by David Doyle

On Deck®

Squadron Signal Publications®

Covers and art by Don Greer
Illustrations by Matheu Spraggins

Introduction

When most people hear "PT boat" the mental image that comes into their minds is that of the 80-foot patrol torpedo boat built by the Electric Launch Company (ELCO) in Bayonne, New Jersey.

These nimble warships, which were built primarily of mahogany planks, not plywood as popular culture believes, by late war delivered the same firepower as had early-war destroyers – but did this at a speed of 40 knots. The high speed was attributed to the trio of Packard marine engines, delivering 1,200 to 1,500 horsepower each, depending on boat class. These V-12s gulped high-octane aviation fuel at the whopping rate of 474 gallons per hour!

Higgins Industries, Huckins Yacht Works, and of course ELCO were makers of PT boats. The earliest of the ELCO boats - 70-foot vessels - were supplied to Great Britain under Lend-Lease. The initial order for 10 such boats was followed by an order for two dozen 77-foot boats. After another order for 24 vessels, and the experience gained from these boats, the 80-footer was born.

In all, 326 of these 80-foot wooden wonders were built, with 296 of them seeing service with the U.S. Navy and the remaining 30 being shipped to the Soviet Union under Lend-Lease.

The PT-565 class boats were the final and hardest hitting of the 80-foot ELCOs (which began with PT-103). The PT 617, shown on these pages, is the sole surviving intact example of these boats. It has been restored and is preserved through the efforts of PT Boats, Inc.

Acknowledgments

This book would not have been possible without the generous assistance of Tom Kailbourn, Scott Taylor, T. Garth Connelly, and especially PT Boats, Inc.

P.T. Boats, Inc. is a 501(c)(3) historical nonprofit organization established in 1946 by veterans of WWII PT service to preserve the history of Patrol Torpedo Boats, their shore bases and tender ships, and the men who manned them. The organization embraces 7,000 PT veterans. PT Boats, Inc., also maintains the PT Boat Museum and Library at Battleship Cove in Fall River, Massachusetts, where more than 4,000 square feet are devoted to 43 commissioned squadrons, some 80 bases and 19 tender ships, including two restored P.T. boats. Supported by tax-deductible contributions, PT Boats, Inc. receives no government funds. Help preserve a piece of American history - the Museum at Battleship Cove, Fall River, Massachusetts. In addition to the 80-foot Elco, PT 617, restored in 1985, visitors can view the 78-foot Higgins, PT 796. Both PTs are National Historic Landmarks. Memorabilia and artifacts from the 45 PT squadrons can also be seen aboard the battleship, USS Massachusetts (BB 59).

PT Boats, Inc.
P. O. Box 38070
Germantown, TN 38133-0070
(901) 755-8440
www.ptboats.org

About the Walk Around®/On Deck Series®

The Walk Around®/On Deck® series is about the details of specific military equipment using color and black-and-white archival photographs and photographs of in-service, preserved, and restored equipment. *Walk Around®* titles are devoted to aircraft and military vehicles, while *On Deck®* titles are devoted to warships. They are picture books of 80 pages, focusing on operational equipment, not one-off or experimental subjects.

Military/Combat Photographs and Snapshots

If you have any photos of aircraft, armor, soldiers, or ships of any nation, particularly wartime snapshots, please share them with us and help make Squadron/Signal's books all the more interesting and complete in the future. Any photograph sent to us will be copied and returned. Electronic images are preferred. The donor will be fully credited for any photos used. Please send them to:

Squadron/Signal Publications
1115 Crowley Drive
Carrollton, TX 75006-1312 U.S.A.
www.SquadronSignalPublications.com

(Title Page) The fast, hard-hitting Elco 80-foot Patrol Torpedo (PT) Boat formed the backbone of the US Navy's mosquito boat fleet during World War II.

(Front Cover) The 585, a late-production ELCO 80-foot PT boat, speeds across a placid surface in the Pacific.

(Back Cover) On the night of 14-15 June, PT 558, along with PTs 552 and 559, fired their torpedoes and sank two enemy corvettes.

PT 103 was the first of the 80-foot ELCO PT boats. It was photographed at the factory of the ELCO Naval Division, Electric Boat Company, at Bayonne, New Jersey on the occasion of its launch in mid-May 1942. Canvas covers envelop the torpedo tubes and machine gun mounts. (PT Boats, Inc.)

PT 117 was photographed during trials at Bayonne on 4 August 1942. Later christened Munda Morn, the boat featured the simple, early-style mast, 21-inch torpedo tubes, two twin .50-caliber machine turrets (sometimes called gun tubs), and a stern-mounted Oerlikon 20mm antiaircraft cannon. (PT Boats, Inc.)

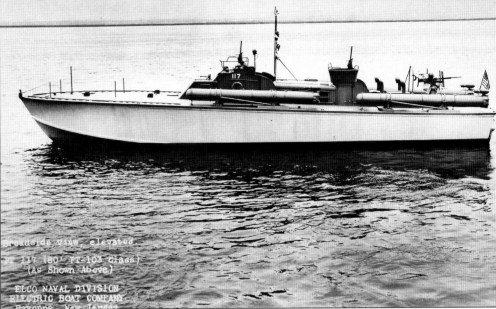

When not in use, the torpedo tubes on ELCO 80-foot PT boats were approximately parallel to the adjacent edge of the hull. The tubes pivoted, and during attacks on enemy shipping, crewmen traversed the fronts of the tubes out using hand cranks inserted into the training gears. The smoke generator was not yet mounted on the stern when the boat was photographed. (PT Boats, Inc.)

A jackstaff has been installed at the center of the foredeck of PT 117. Flanking the jackstaff are lifelines made of wire rope and supported by two stanchions on each side. Crewmen could hang onto those lifelines when the boat was running at speed or travelling on rough water. (PT Boats, Inc.)

PT 117 was part of the PT-103 class. From 1942 to 1945, 326 of these craft were built. The shape of the hull and cabin remained virtually unchanged throughout the production run. (PT Boats, Inc.)

The 80-foot ELCOs were built by setting the prefabricated bulkheads into a jig, installing the keel, chines (the frame where the bottom and sides of the hull meet), and longitudinal and diagonal battens. At the stage of construction shown here, workmen have started installing the first layer of 6-foot x 1-foot mahogany hull planks. Those planks were then covered with a layer of aircraft fabric impregnated with marine glue. Finally, a top layer of mahogany planks was laid diagonally across the first plank layer. (PT Boats, Inc.)

On 20 August 1942, a U.S. Navy photographer snapped a series of photos of what would become the most famous PT boat of all, PT 109, to illustrate the manner of securing a PT boat to the deck of a transport ship. The craft was stored on the shelter deck of the SS Joseph Stanton at Norfolk Navy Yard. (PT Boats, Inc.)

PT 109 was placed in a form-fitting cradle. Cables attached to beams placed across the deck held down the boat securely in the cradle. (PT Boats, Inc.)

The aft end of PT 109 is seen aboard the Joseph Stanton. The ship would soon transport PT 109 and other craft of Squadron 5 to the Panama Canal, the interim station where the squadron was assigned before shipping off to the Solomon Islands. There are canvas covers over both ends of the torpedo tubes, the 20mm cannon, and the .50-caliber turrets. (PT Boats, Inc.)

PT 107 was photographed while on duty with Squadron 5 in the Panama Canal Zone. In place of the two aft torpedo tubes, it has been fitted with four depth charge racks and two storage boxes on each side. PT 107 was later destroyed in an accidental fire on 18 June 1944. (PT Boats, Inc.)

An ELCO 80-footer sails at speed. This boat is armed with 37mm and 20mm automatic cannons and two 5-inch rocket launchers on the foredeck, two .50-caliber machine guns in tub mounts, Mk 13 torpedoes, and a 40mm Bofors gun on the aft deck. The boat sports the late-type SO-3 radar mast introduced in 1945, and a canopy has been rigged over the bridge. (PT Boats, Inc.)

As seen in a wartime color photograph of a PT boat, PT 132, nicknamed Little Lulu, served with Squadron (or, Ron) 7 in the southwest Pacific. Its original mast has been replaced with the SO-3 type introduced in 1945, with the radome removed, exposing the antenna proper. Armaments include a 37mm and a 20mm cannon on the foredeck, an eight-round Mk 50 5-inch rocket launcher on either side of the cabin, and Mk 13 torpedoes in the aft racks. There is a canvas top over the bridge. (PT Boats, Inc.)

A sailor is sitting on his boat's starboard eight-tube 5-inch rocket launcher, swung out into position for use. These launchers considerably increased the boat's firepower. (PT Boats, Inc.)

PT 333 was cruising at moderate speed when this photograph was taken. A sailor is manning the 20mm automatic cannon on the foredeck, to the side of which is stored a dinghy. Both torpedo tubes are empty, a possible indication that the boat was not in a combat area. The radar mast is retracted and there is a searchlight to the left of the radio mast. (PT Boats, Inc.)

PT 579 was one of the 60 ELCO 80-foot PT boats manufactured in 1945. This photo shows it painted in a Measure 31, Design 20L camouflage scheme with four colors: Outside Green 2, Outside Green 3, Deck Green (the deck was painted in this color only), and Black. There are 37mm ammunition storage boxes to the rear of the 37mm gun. Port covers installed on the windows in the front of the chart house (also called the radio room, chart cabin, or the chart and radio cabin) conceal the light inside the boat from aircraft passing overhead. (PT Boats, Inc.)

PT 579 has pulled abreast of the photographer's boat in this view. She carried a typical late-World War II armament suite of 20mm, 37mm, 40mm, and .50-caliber guns and 5-inch rocket launchers. The barrel of the 40mm gun is lowered onto a rest on top of the limit stop (also called the pipe railstop), a frame intended to deflect the gunners from unintentionally shooting up the cabin, bridge, torpedo tubes, or mast during the heat of combat. (PT Boats, Inc.)

The engine exhausts are being expelled through the six external mufflers on the transom, exiting below the water, thus churning up the water. For high-speed operation, the mufflers were bypassed, with the exhaust being expelled through ports immediately above the mufflers. (PT Boats, Inc.)

Steel rope life lines are rigged to the stanchions of PT 588, and the barrel of the 40mm Bofors gun is in its rest atop the limit stop. To the front of the limit stop is the engine room hatch, with a 40mm ammunition locker to the rear of the hatch. Stored on top of the cabin is a dinghy. (PT Boats, Inc.)

PT 588 was commissioned 10 April 1945. As seen from a dockside, her Mk 50 rocket launchers are in their inboard stored position. Resting on its mount near the bow is the 37mm automatic cannon, with its 30-round magazine on top. This gun was originally used in the P-39 fighter, but it was well adapted for mounting on the decks of PT boats and used for barge-busting operations. Also visible are the anchor, the several hull vents along the edge of the deck, the various ammunition lockers on the foredeck, and the life raft stored atop the chart house. (PT Boats, Inc.)

The crews of the 40mm and .50-caliber antiaircraft guns man their weapons as PT 596 proceeds at low speed. The Mk 50 rocket launchers are swung out for action. They were rotated inboard for reloading or storing when not in action. Note the late-model mast and the placement of the smoke generator on the starboard side of the after deck. (PT Boats, Inc.)

Armed with Mk 13 torpedoes, PT 603 clips along at a high rate of speed outside of an active combat zone, as evidenced by the covers over the guns and the radar antenna. The 20mm gun has been removed from its mount to the rear of the 37mm cannon. (PT Boats, Inc.)

PT 617 is preserved at the PT Boat Museum at Battleship Cove, Fall River, Massachusetts. Nicknamed Dragon Lady, the boat failed to see combat during WWII but was used for training and as a diving platform in Florida. PT Boats, Inc., purchased the deteriorating boat, and after restoration, it was placed on display at Battleship Cove in 1986. It is on the National Historic Register and is the only fully restored ELCO PT boat on public display in the world.

The mooring bit is secured to the deck with slotted screws.

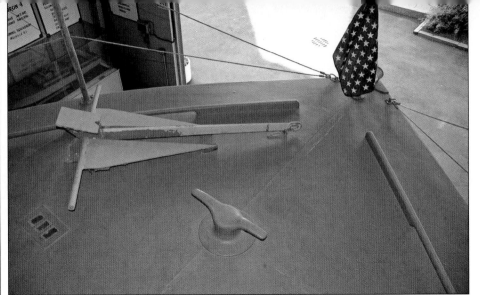

The anchor is stored on the deck at the bow. To the lower left is one of a number of deadlights on the deck. These are mini-skylights set in protective frames. On the centerline of the deck is a mooring bit, also known as a Sampson post. A jack staff is attached to the bow.

Steel rope lifelines are attached to stanchions and are secured to eyes on the deck at the bow. Toe rails are situated on either side of the bow, parallel with the edge of the deck.

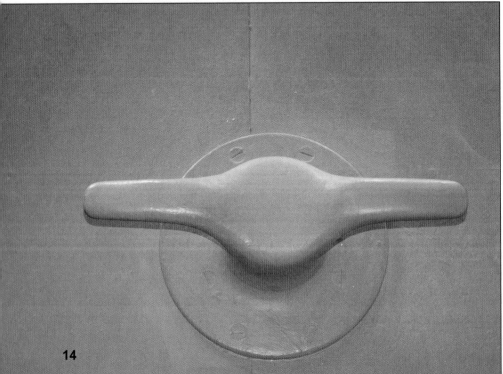

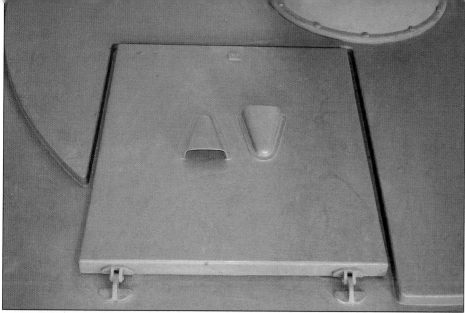

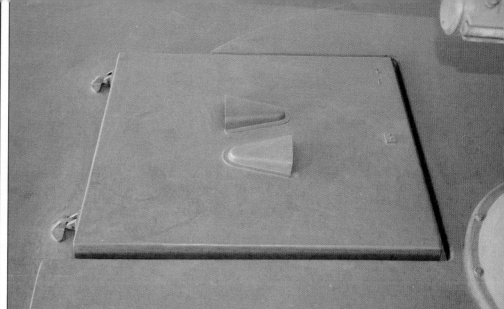

The forehatch has fore- and aft-pointing scoop vents and is hinged on the forward side. The circular platform for the 37mm cannon mount, called a gun-working circle, is fitted around the hatch; the base of the mount is at the upper right.

The forehatch is seen here from the compartment below. There is a latch to the left and the vent openings can be seen towards the center of the hatch.

A side view of the hatch. All hatches on the ELCO 80-footers were to be of cast aluminum with raised gaskets.

Late in World War II, Oldsmobile M9 37mm automatic cannons were installed using the M1 37mm gun mount attached to a reinforced portion of the foredeck of ELCO 80-footers. Behind the gun are two 37mm ammunition lockers.

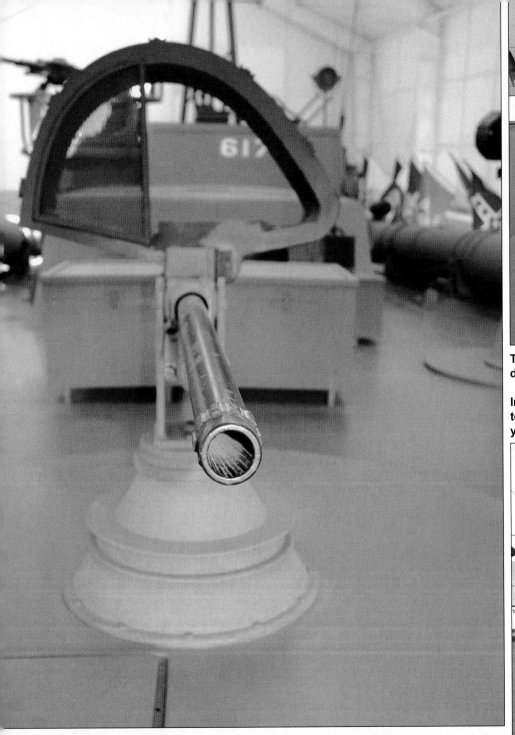

The rifling is clearly visible inside the muzzle of the M9 37mm gun.

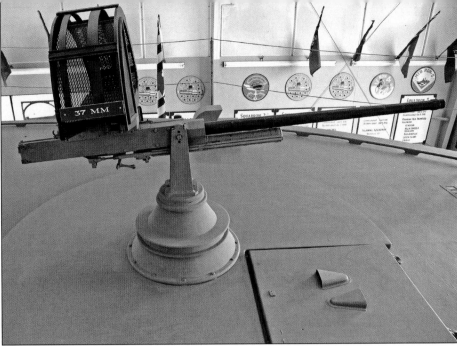

The M9 cannon would have been equipped with hand grips at the rear of the receiver during WWII service.

In service, 30 rounds of 37mm ammunition would have been fed into the magazine on top of the gun. The gun could fire up to 125 rounds per minute to a range of 8,875 yards.

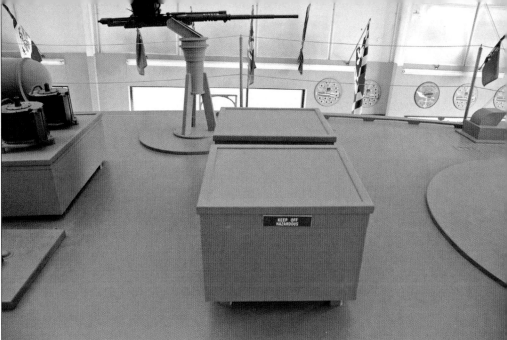

The 37mm ammunition lockers appear in this photograph directed toward the rear of the boat. Several designs of lockers for this type of ammunition were used on ELCO 80-foot PT boats.

There are three hinges on the rear of each of the 37mm ammunition lockers. To the far right is a deck vent with internal blower.

The 37mm ammunition lockers are seen here from the side, with a 20mm automatic antiaircraft gun on a tripod mount behind them. To the left is a locker for 20mm ammunition, with two 20mm magazines on top.

Above this deck vent on the port side of the bow are a toe rail and the base of a lifeline stanchion.

Rust staining can be seen on the inside of the deck vent. To the upper left is a deadlight.

The addition of the 20mm and 37mm automatic cannons on the bow of later-production ELCO 80-foot PT boats was a radical departure from the clean foredecks of the early-production boats. The added weaponry transformed these craft into gunboats, capable of engaging enemy shore targets as well as light shipping, and these boats could venture close inshore where destroyers and larger gunboats never could.

PT 617 has a 20mm automatic antiaircraft gun on a tripod mount to the port side of the foredeck. An ammunition magazine is inserted into the receiver of the gun, while two other magazines are atop the 20mm ammunition locker in front of the chart house.

This 20mm gun is mounted on a simplified replica tripod mount. A grab handle was incorporated into the front and rear of each 20mm magazine. There is a hatch to the left of the photo, and the torpedo tube training gear is visible inboard of the 21-inch torpedo tube. PT 617 originally was equipped with Mk 13 torpedoes on racks.

The 20mm magazines each held 60 rounds. With the 20mm gun's rate of fire of 480 rounds per minute, it was necessary to fire short bursts, and loaders were kept busy mounting fresh magazines onto the piece.

Ready magazines sit atop the 20mm ammunition locker, seen here from behind. Gaskets in the lids made the lockers watertight. Each could hold three magazines. On the deck to the lower right is the inboard edge of the hatch, with the rear hinge showing.

Two 20mm magazines sit on ready racks atop the 20mm ammunition locker. Some photos of wartime ELCO 80-foot PT boats show three ready racks for magazines on top of the locker. The magazines have Parkerized finishes.

There are windows on the front of the chart house and a deadlight on the roof of that cabin. Toward the upper right of the photograph is the inboard side of the port navigation light mounting panel.

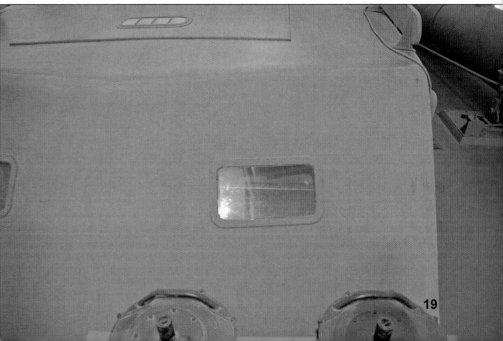

19

The 37mm gun mount and ready ammunition lockers, chart house, bridge, radar mast, and starboard .50-caliber machine gun turret are viewed from low on the starboard side of the deck near the bow. To the far left is the starboard forward torpedo tube.

The craft's number, 617, is painted on the coaming of the bridge in white with black shading. The panel on the chart house roof was designed to be removable, to allow for the removal of a 200-gallon potable water tank below the chart house floor if necessary.

PT 545 was completed on 8 September 1944. In this view, a life raft is stored on top of the chart house. At the left of the chart house is a BN directional antenna. To the right of the raft are the UHF antenna and the shortwave whip antenna. The mast is of the type installed on PTs 486 to 563 (and retrofitted on some earlier ELCO 80-footers) and includes a radome on top. To the left is the covered muzzle of a mortar mounted on the foredeck. (PT Boats, Inc.)

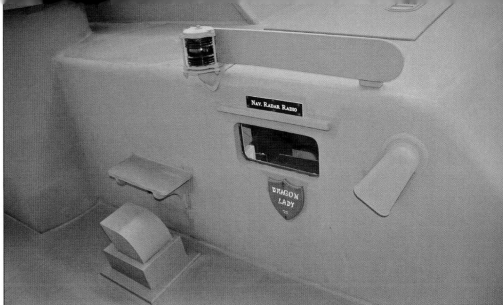

The chart house is constructed of plywood over a wooden frame structure. To the lower left is the starboard navigation light, and to the other side of the chart house roof is the rear of the mounting panel for the port navigation light. The purpose of these panels was to make only that particular navigation light (and not the different colored light on the opposite side of the chart house) visible to other craft.

The starboard navigation light had a green glass lens while the navigation light on the port side of the vessel was red in accordance with international conventions designed to help ships determine direction and right-of-way and avoid collisions.

On the starboard side of the chart room, the navigation light and mounting panel are to the top, and a vent is to the front of the window. The escutcheon below the window bears the boat's nickname: *Dragon Lady*. Over the deck hull vent is a built-in step.

This view of an ELCO 80-foot PT boat tied up at a dock displays details of the Mk 50 5-inch rocket launcher in its stored position, with no rockets loaded. The launcher swung out for firing; it could be elevated, while traverse was achieved by aiming the boat at the azimuth of the target. To the rear of the launcher is a drop rack for a torpedo. A shuttered hood covers the chart house window. (PT Boats, Inc.)

21

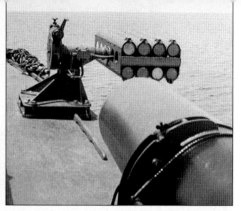

Two Elco 80-foot PT boats with Mk 50 rocket launchers speed across the surface. The launcher's pedestal and elevating gear were identical on both sides of the boat, so the elevating crank was in the front of the port side mount and behind the starboard side mount (as seen here) when swung out for firing. The ignition cable is plugged into a receptacle on the deck. (PT Boats, Inc.)

This wartime photograph shows a starboard Mk 50 launcher, fully loaded and deployed for firing. In addition to the rockets loaded into the tubes, a complete reload of 16 more rocket rounds was stored onboard those boats that were equipped with the launchers. Behind the launcher, at the lower right of the picture, is the front end of a Mk 13 torpedo. (PT Boats, Inc.)

This photo of the port Mk 50 launcher taken during World War II shows the electrical ignition cable attached; the launchers were fired from the bridge. The round mechanism is the elevating gear; on top of it are the elevating crank and locking knob. On the side of the gear is an elevation scale and indicator. The lever below and to the right of the gear locks the launcher tubes into position parallel to the centerline of the boat. Igniters are visible on top of and below the left side of the launcher-tubes assembly. (PT Boats, Inc.)

Two sailors brandish spin-stabilized 5-inch rockets while loading a Mk 50 launcher. Only the two upper right tubes remain to be loaded. The launcher is deployed in its launching position, outboard of the deck; normally, the tubes would be loaded with the launcher in its stored position. (PT Boats, Inc.)

Missing from its mount on the port side of the chart house is the red navigation light. The mount for the whip antenna is to the side of the bridge. A deck vent and several deadlights are on the deck.

The forward support, or saddle, of the torpedo tube rests on the training gear, while the rear support rests on a pivot. The dome-shaped cover secured over the front of the torpedo tube was removed when preparing to fire the torpedo. At the lower front of the tube, the holes in the plate aligned with the triangular locking bracket attached to the deck when the tube is in either the stored or firing positions. A locking pin inserted through either hole in the plate and the locking bracket secured the tube in place.

The training gear is seen here from forward. The horizontal "rod" is a transverse screw that traversed the saddle of the tube in a curved channel mounted on the deck. A hand crank, usually stored on the roof of the day cabin (or day room), was fitted vertically over the stud at the top of the gearbox to operate the training gear.

The forward saddle and training gear are seen here from the inboard side, with the curved traverse channel on the base of the mount visible below the saddle. The tubes fitted to early PT boats were trained outward for firing so that the torpedoes would clear the deck. The forward tubes swung out about 8 degrees, and the rear tubes about 12 degrees, the extra angle being necessary for the torpedoes to clear the forward tubes.

Another view of the forward saddle and training gear, emphasizing the curved traverse channel and bracing of the torpedo tube.

The port-side vent is seen here from the side in its position next to the bridge, its aperture facing aft.

The deck vent/blower and deadlights are seen inboard of the port torpedo tube.

The deadlights in the deck on the port side of the bridge provide lighting for the commander's cabin, officers' head, and officers' cabin. The forward base of the torpedo mount is on the left and the 20mm gun's tripod mount is visible in the background.

The bench on the bulkhead behind the port side of the bridge is seen in this view facing forward. At lower right is the forward port corner of the day cabin with a toe rail on its roof.

This ammunition locker is on the port side of the engine room hatch. To the left is the rear bulkhead of the day cabin, with an access hatch (according to the specifications, wide enough to accommodate a patient on a stretcher) to the starboard.

The port torpedo tube is viewed here from aft. The cylinder on top of the rear of the tube is the impulse unit. A small explosive charge inserted into the unit was ignited when the torpedo was fired, expelling the projectile from the tube. To the right of the tube are the day cabin with a toe rail along its roof, a deck vent/blower, and part of the port machine gun turret.

The forward side of the day cabin has a window and a storage box.

The engine room hatch is viewed here from the port side. The curved section to the top is the scoop for the engine room ventilator. Braces for the limit stop for the 40mm gun are fastened to the sides of the scoop.

A grab handle and internal bracing are visible on the open engine room hatch. A raised coaming surrounds the edge of the opening.

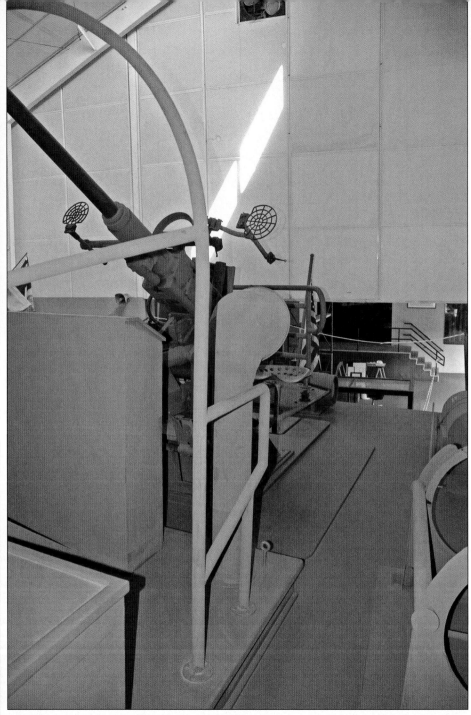

Aft of the engine room hatch/vent is the front side of the 40mm ammunition locker (far left), the limit stop, a cowl vent, and the 40mm gun.

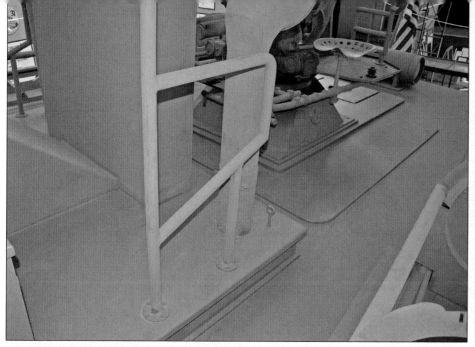

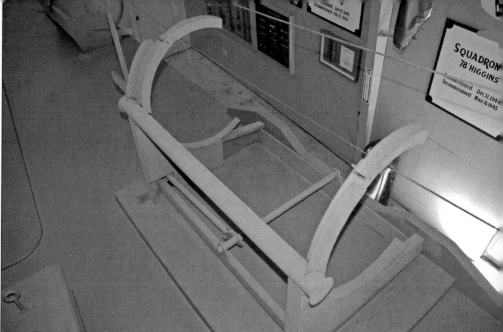

The engine room hatch, ammunition locker, limit stop, and cowl vents are attached to the engine room deck, which is a removable cover (note the lifting eye at the corner).

The port torpedo rack is seen here from aft with the engine room deck visible to the right.

PT 617 was originally fitted with racks for Mk 13 torpedoes. These racks are retained in the aft positions. The Mk 13 torpedoes could not be launched electrically from the bridge. Instead, a crewman started the torpedo's motor and gyros by pulling a lever and launched the torpedo by pulling a second lever. With motor and propeller running, the torpedo slid down the lower, greased rails of the rack and entered the water.

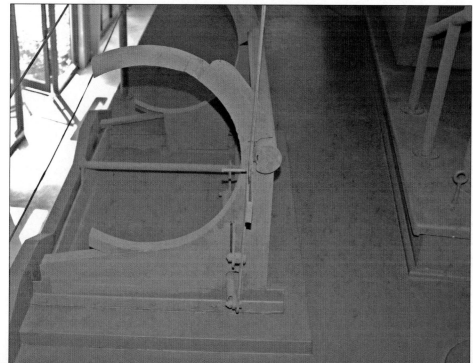

Bofors 40mm

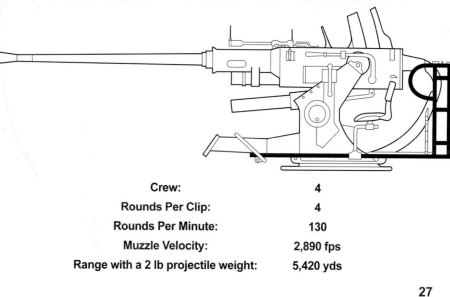

Crew:	4
Rounds Per Clip:	4
Rounds Per Minute:	130
Muzzle Velocity:	2,890 fps
Range with a 2 lb projectile weight:	5,420 yds

The 40mm gun mount as viewed from the aft port corner of the deck. The tractor-type seat of the vertical gun pointer is to the lower center of the photo. The gun operator fired the weapon using the right pedal. The lateral gun pointer sat to the other side of the gun and traversed the piece. The gun mount's guard rail is to the left. Forward of the gun is the 40mm ammunition locker, which could hold 64 rounds in four-round clips.

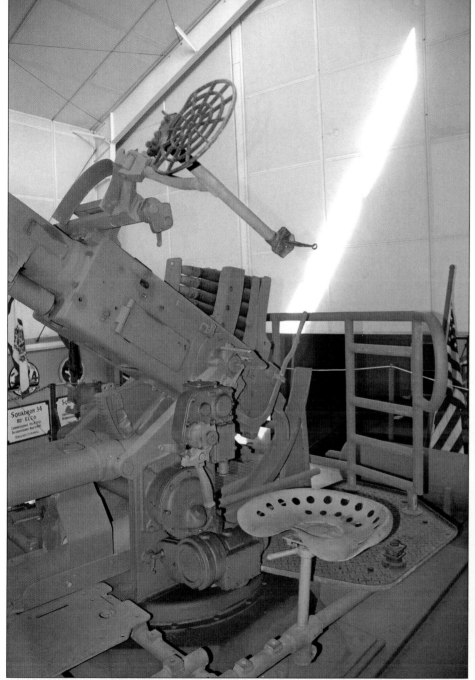

The gun loader would stand on the tread-plate platform provided on the 40mm mount and insert four-round clips into the weapon as needed. In the photo, clipped rounds are visible in the feed hopper. At the top of the photograph is the vertical gun pointer's ring sight.

The 40mm gun and mount are viewed here from aft. At the breech end of the receiver of the gun (lower center) is the spent-casing ejector port and curved deflector, below which is the spent-casing chute. The barrel is resting on the barrel rest on top of the limit stop. The contours of the top rail of the limit stop are asymmetrical.

A roll-off depth-charge rack is mounted on the aft port side of PT 617.

The depth charge and rack are seen here from the side, facing forward.

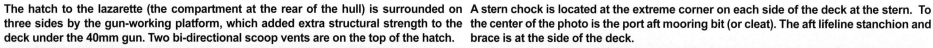

The hatch to the lazarette (the compartment at the rear of the hull) is surrounded on three sides by the gun-working platform, which added extra structural strength to the deck under the 40mm gun. Two bi-directional scoop vents are on the top of the hatch.

A stern chock is located at the extreme corner on each side of the deck at the stern. To the center of the photo is the port aft mooring bit (or cleat). The aft lifeline stanchion and brace is at the side of the deck.

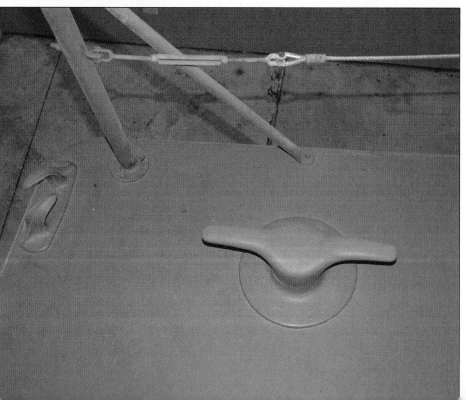

A smoke generator Mk 6 was specified for use on PT 617. This Mk 6 is mounted on the vessel's stern. When the titanium tetrachloride in the generator was released and introduced into the atmosphere, it formed a thick fog.

There is a valve within the nozzle of the smoke generator. A crewman gave the valve three full turns to open it, thus initiating a smoke screen. An ensign staff is attached to the center of the deck at the stern.

The smoke generator consists of a 35-gallon steel bottle containing pressurized titanium tetrachloride, which would be expelled through a nozzle at one end of the bottle. Late-model ELCO 80-foot PT boats generally had an ELCO-made smoke generator that consisted of a separate tank mounted on a wooden cradle and strapped to the deck.

A side view of the lazarette hatch appears in this picture, with the smoke discharger and stern to the left and loader's platform of the 40mm gun to right.

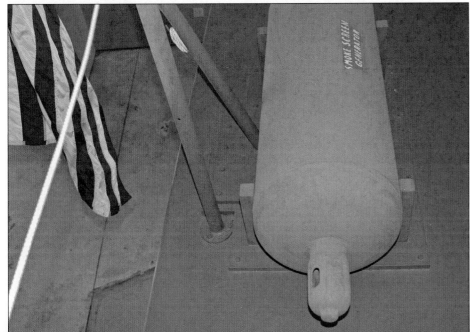

The lateral pointer's seat and footrests on the 40mm gun mount are in the lower center. A tubular lateral frame holds both of the pointers' ring sights. There is a conical flash suppressor at the muzzle of the gun.

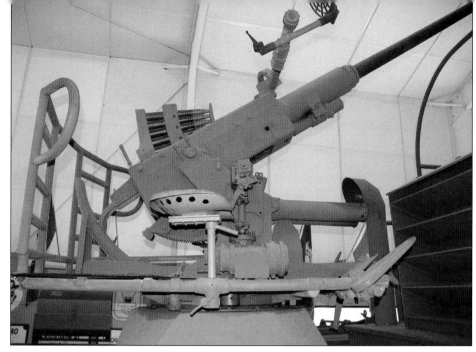

The lateral pointer's seat is adjustable forward and aft by loosening the clamp at the pedestal's base. To the rear of the receiver is the curved spent-casing deflector, while the large, curved object below it is the spent-shell chute. Projecting horizontally from the front of the gun carriage are the two equilibrator cylinders.

Viewing the 40mm gun from the front, the elevating gear and equilibrators are at the center, within the carriage. To the left is the traversing mechanism, and to the right the elevating mechanism. In action, the gun layers would have operated their respective mechanisms with hand cranks.

To the rear of the equilibrator cylinders under the centerline of the gun's receiver is the elevating gear. The gun barrel is air-cooled.

The gearbox, to which the lateral pointer's hand crank would have been attached, is to the lower left in this photo. The starboard side of the 40mm receiver is to the upper left. The tube projecting below the equilibrator cylinders is the spent casing chute; as the gun was fired, empty casings were ejected from the rear of the receiver, traveled down the chute, and dropped onto the deck to the front of the gun. The 40mm ammunition locker is to the center, with the .50-caliber turrets in the background.

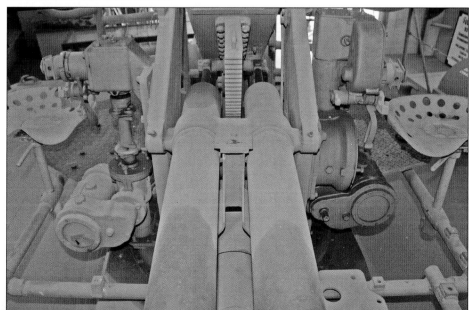

The mast, with a radome atop it, is on the forward end of the day cabin roof. The mast was collapsible, as seen from the hinges at the bottom of its legs. When folded, it rested on the support in the foreground. A hatch is at the far starboard side of the cabin roof.

The mast from aft, with the mast support at the bottom of the photo. The mast is of the intermediate type that was used on PTs 486 to 563. The radome at top housed a Raytheon SO surface search radar antenna.

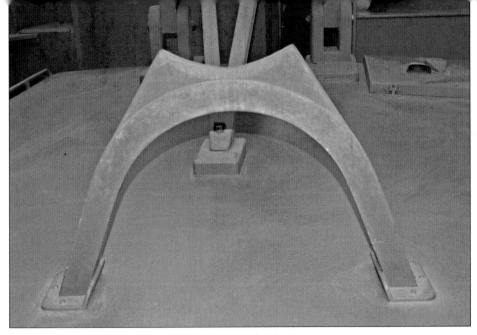

Details of the mast rest and brace are seen in this image.

On the back of the starboard side of the day cabin is the aft hatch, seen to the far left of the photo. There is a vent on the deck next to the cabin and to the right of the picture is the starboard torpedo tube. The starboard .50-caliber turret is in the background. The lower part of the turret is scooped to provide more room for the crew to negotiate the narrow space between the tub and the torpedo mount.

The inboard side of the port turret is seen from the starboard rear corner of the day cabin. The turrets were made from molded fabricated plywood and mounted a scarf ring gun mount for twin .50-caliber machine guns. Above the top of the turret are the gunner's back rest and the limit stop, a tubular frame designed to keep the gunner from hitting his own boat.

The aft hatch is located on the rear starboard side of the day cabin.

The engine air intake vent is to the rear of the open engine room hatch. Incorporated into the interior of the air intake are light baffles, water traps, a hinged shutter, and drains.

The deck ventilator located near the aft end of the starboard side of the day cabin. A torpedo tube is in the background to the right.

The deck ventilator on the starboard side of the day cabin is seen here from the side.

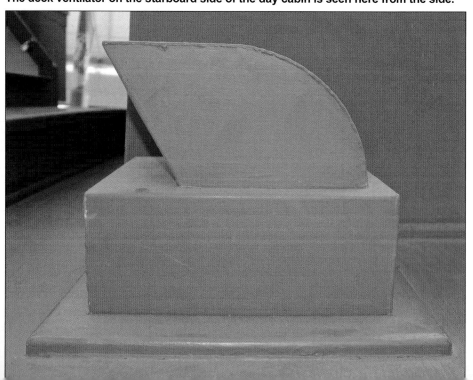

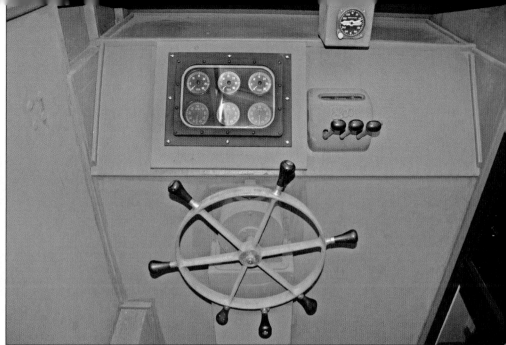

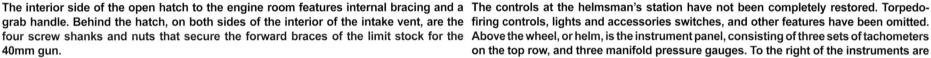

The interior side of the open hatch to the engine room features internal bracing and a grab handle. Behind the hatch, on both sides of the interior of the intake vent, are the four screw shanks and nuts that secure the forward braces of the limit stock for the 40mm gun.

In addition to the six handles at the ends of the spokes, the wheel has one perpendicular handle for fast turning. Inside the housing to which the wheel is attached is a roller chain that transfers the movements of the wheel to a steering gear below the deck. While later PT boats had metal wheels, as here, the early boats featured a more traditional wooden wheel.

The controls at the helmsman's station have not been completely restored. Torpedo-firing controls, lights and accessories switches, and other features have been omitted. Above the wheel, or helm, is the instrument panel, consisting of three sets of tachometers on the top row, and three manifold pressure gauges. To the right of the instruments are the throttle controls, with "ELCO" embossed in script on the housing. A compass is mounted on the inside of the coaming.

The helmsman's compartment is the only part of the ELCO 80-foot PT boats that has armor-plate protection. Several compasses would have been mounted in the compartment, none of which, reportedly, were very accurate.

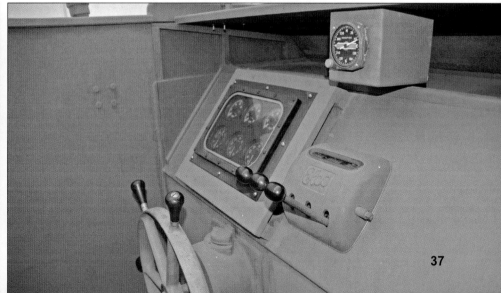

To the starboard side of the bridge is a shelf, below which is the open hatch to the chart room.

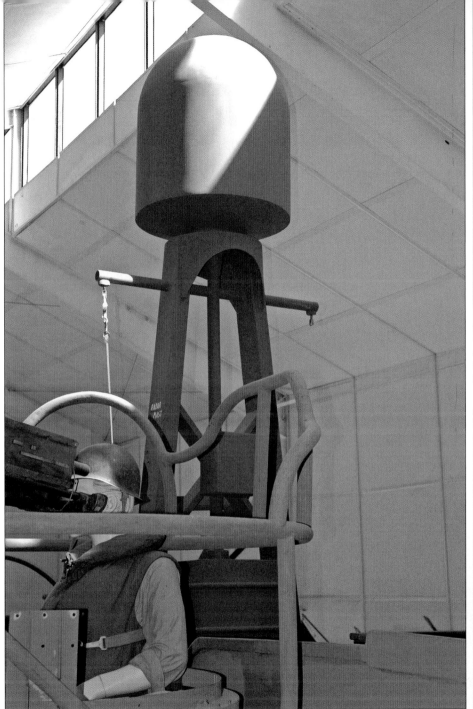

The mast and radome appear here as viewed from the front of the starboard turret, which is manned by a mannequin.

Although not installed in this view, each late-war ELCO 80-foot PT boat was supplied with a canvas cover for both turrets, as well as canvas spray shields, to be installed between the top of the turret and the limit stop.

A shot shows the top of the mast and the radome with a searchlight and whip antenna to the right.

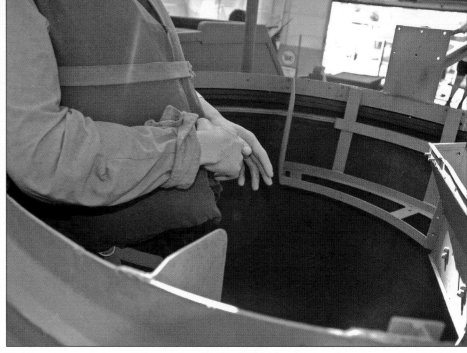

Turret diameter on the PT 617 was 48 inches, as it was on all PTs from 565 to 624. Their plywood was 3/4 of an inch thick. The machine gun mounts in this production run of ELCO 80-foot PT boats were designated Mk. 17 Mod. 1. The limit stops were fabricated from brass or steel tubing.

To the front of the scarf ring is a collection bin for spent cartridges and links. Extending above the ring is the pedestal on which the .50-caliber machine guns are mounted.

The hand-operated scarf ring and racks for .50-caliber ammunition boxes (not installed here) are visible inside the .50-caliber turret. The government provided the scarf rings to ELCO for installation on the turrets.

The pintle and buffered cradle assembly are visible on the underside of the PT 617's .50 caliber M2HB machine guns. Missing parts include the grips, triggers, and flexible feed chutes.

A sailor mans the starboard twin air-cooled .50-caliber machine guns aboard a Higgins-built PT in this color photograph from World War II. The curved grips allowed the gunner to achieve extreme elevation of the guns—a difficult thing to do with smaller hand grips. The linked ammunition entered a flexible chute that helped guide the constantly flexing ammunition belts into the feed without jamming. (Naval Historical Center)

Interior Compartments

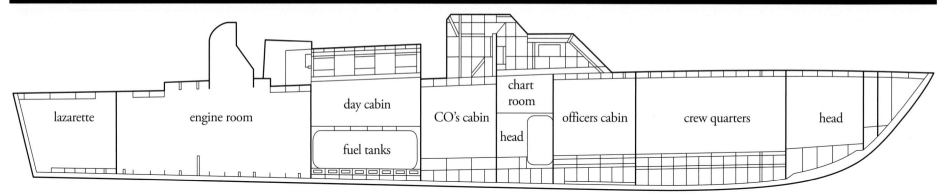

80' 70' 60' 50' 40' 30' 20' 10' 0'

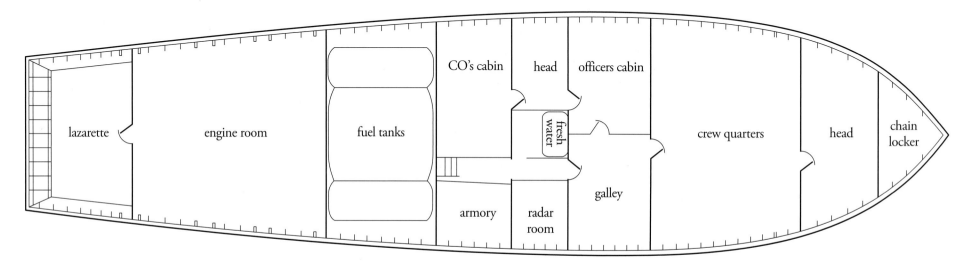

Camouflage Pattern

The camouflage pattern applied to PT boats differed from side to side. PT-596 was painted in a scheme known as Measure 31, Camouflage Design 20L. This scheme included Deck Green (20-G) (on some of the horizontal surfaces), Ocean Green (5-OG - light green) and Navy Green (5-NG - dark green).

The rear of the impulse unit is located atop the breech cover, an inboard-hinged assembly that is held in place by eight wing nuts. The cover is well braced to withstand the pressures of the explosive charges.

The training gear, nose cap, and locking bracket are evident in this view of the starboard torpedo tube. The lower side of the turret adjacent to the torpedo tube is scooped.

The impulse unit on the upper aft end of the starboard torpedo is seen in this view, facing aft. In the event of an electrical misfire during a torpedo launch, a crewman would hit a striker on the rear of the unit with a mallet, manually igniting the explosive charge inside, which then propelled the torpedo out of the tube.

The impulse unit is seen from the inboard side.

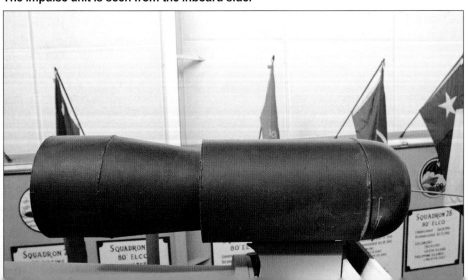

Several plates screwed on to the top of the torpedo tube allow access to torpedo components.

The brace rod appears to the left in this view of the inboard side of the aft saddle of the starboard torpedo tube. The saddle rests on a turntable, allowing the rear of the tube to pivot when the front end was swung out for firing.

The aft saddle and brace are seen here from the front.

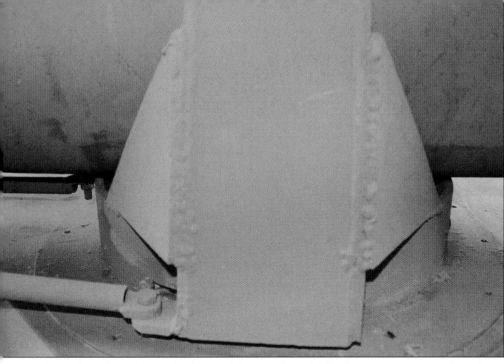

The aft starboard torpedo tube saddle together with its brace rod are seen here from the side.

The training gear, attached to the forward starboard torpedo tube saddle, appear in this photograph from a slightly different angle that shows the gearbox, transverse screw, and curved traversing channel.

The training gear is seen here attached to the forward starboard torpedo tube saddle.

A welded steel towing eye and pad were fixed to the stems of late-model ELCO 80-foot PT boats just above the waterline at the bow. The assembly was hot dipped and galvanized. Extra blocking and brackets inside the hull further strengthened the attachment point. The assembly facilitated high-speed towing if the boat were disabled.

The towing eye is viewed from above and over the starboard side.

The chines appear in this close-up photograph of the stem of the PT 617. The chine is the structural member where the top of the hull joins the bottom of the hull.

This view of the towing eye, taken from slightly underneath, also shows the joints between the hull planks.

The towing eye and pad are seen here on the port side of the PT 617.

The port torpedo tube and 20mm cannon of PT 617 are seen here from below. Visible above the tube to the right are the searchlight and whip antenna.

The radome and mast, torpedo tube, and turret are seen from below in this view of the middle section of the port side of the hull. To the far right are the aft stop limit and the barrel of the 40mm gun.

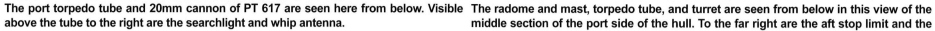

This archival photograph of a wartime ELCO PT boat's mufflers shows the butterfly valve linkages and valves. The linkages opened the valves (as seen here) when the boat was operating at high speed, thus bypassing the mufflers. The camouflage paint has been applied to the mufflers.

Immediately to the front of the ensign staff at the stern of PT 617 is the smoke generator. The six mufflers are arrayed on the stern, but the linkages for the butterfly valves for the bypass outlets (at the top of each muffler) are not installed.

The government supplied six propellers per ELCO PT boat: three to be installed on the shafts, and three to be stored as spares. The planking in the wooden construction of the vessel is clearly visible.

Propellers were made of an aluminum-manganese-bronze alloy and were right-hand turning, with a diameter of approximately 30 inches.

Noise vs. Horsepower

Linkages connect exhaust cutouts to the mufflers. Opening the valves allowed the exhaust to exit directly to the atmosphere. The reduced exhaust back pressure greatly increased the horsepower delivered by the engines, at the cost of greatly increased exhaust noise.

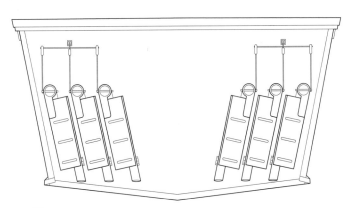

Bridge

The commander on the bridge (left) of an ELCO 80-foot PT boat could easily direct the forward .50 caliber machine gunner (right).

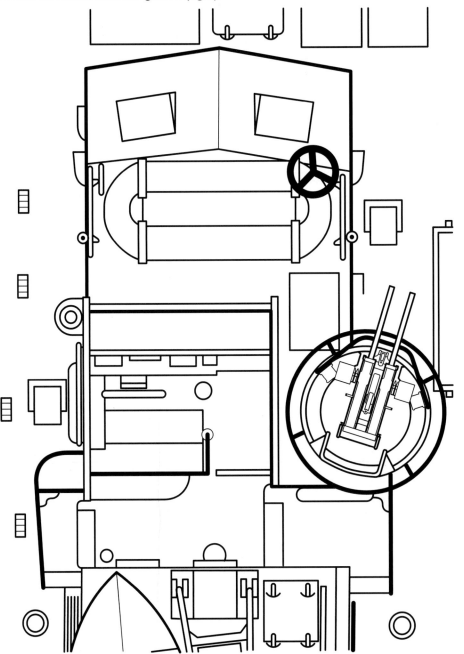

The chart house is seen here through the open hatch from the bridge. On the opposite (front) side of the narrow red bulkhead is a fixed seat on the starboard side of the cabin.

To the front of the radar console is the starboard front window of the chart house. To the left is a compass, below which is an open navigational instruments case.

A plywood table is built into the front and sides of the chart house, at the same level as the deck outside. To the left is a radar console. In the center is a Type CMX-46159 radio receiver. Above the window is a swing-down blackout blind. There is a round vent hole at the upper front corner of the cabin's sidewall (upper left of photo).

There is a fixed seat with a tubular armrest on the starboard side of the chart house.

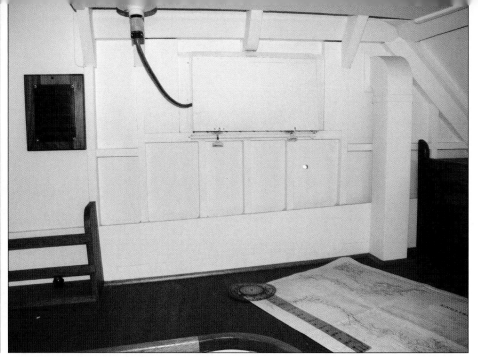

A cabinet with several sets of drawers extends a little more than halfway across the table at the front of the chart house. The construction of the superstructure is plywood over wood frame. Interior surfaces of the hull and deck houses were painted with a primer and two coats of a fire-retardant white paint.

The port blackout blind of the chart house is secured in the lowered position.

On the port side of the table in the chart house is a rack to store books and oddments. A commemorative plaque is mounted on the wall.

The panel in the roof of the chart house was designed to be removable in case there is a need to remove the potable water tank located below the chart house floor. In the panel is a deadlight with a blackout shutter.

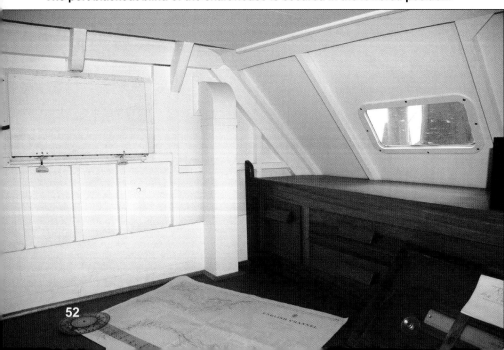

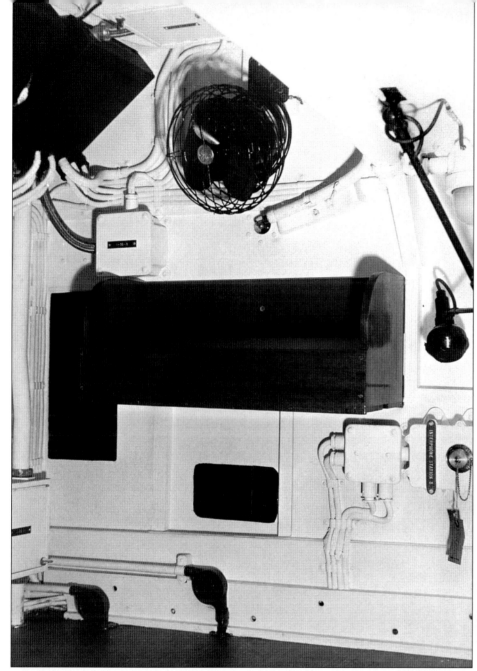

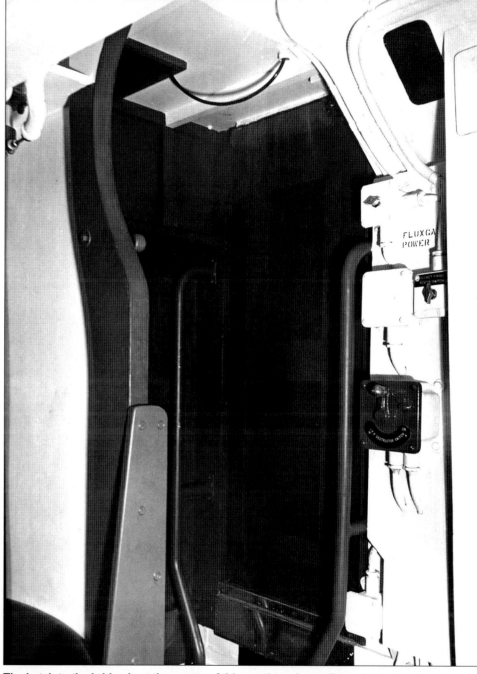

The side table is at the bottom in this archival photo of the port aft corner of the chart house aboard an ELCO 80-foot PT boat. Features appearing in the picture include an electric fan, electrical conduits and junction boxes, and a bookshelf. The box located toward the lower right of the photograph is labeled "Intercom Station 5." (PT Boats, Inc.)

The hatch to the bridge is at the center of this wartime photo of the aft starboard corner of the chart house. To the left is the side frame of the built-in chair. Mounted on the bulkhead at right are the destructor switch for the Identification, Friend or Foe (IFF) set and, above it, power switches for the flux gate: electronic equipment associated with the remote-indicating magnetic compass. (PT Boats, Inc.)

The galley is starboard of the centerline of the boat, below the front half of the chart house. As originally outfitted, it had a porcelain-enamel sink, aluminum sink drain, a refrigerator (including an evaporator unit with four ice trays), and a main food compartment.

Specifications for late-model ELCO 80-foot PT boats called for cupboards of western red cedar with door frames of mahogany to be installed below the sink board and counter.

A World War II photograph taken next to the ladder leading up to the chart house shows the passageway through a watertight hatch into the galley. (PT Boats, Inc.)

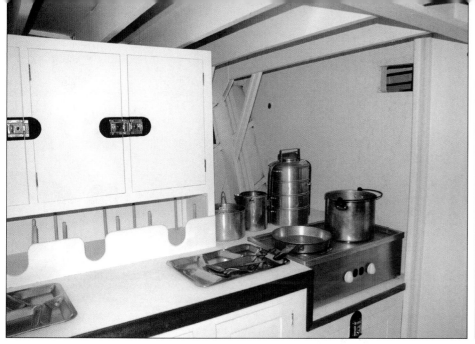

Inset into the end of the counter toward the aft end of the galley is a small electric stove. The 1944 specifications for late-model ELCO 80-foot PT boats called for a portable oven, supplied with the stove, to be stored on a shelf above the stove. Also included with the stove were assorted pots, pans, a coffee pot, strainers, and pot holders.

In this archival photo, the door to the compartment under the sink is open to the left. The hand pump that drew water for the sink can be seen to the far left. To the right, the two doors of the refrigerator are open. Ice trays can be seen in the refrigerator compartment to the right. (PT Boats, Inc.)

Many of the earlier 103-series boats were painted Dark Gray (5-D) on the deck and topsides, while the hull was finished in Navy Gray #5 above the waterline. The bottom of the boat was painted with three coats of a proprietary product known as Copperoyd.

The crew quarters occupy the width of the boat, below the foredeck, forward of the galley and the officers' cabin. This view, from the center of the compartment, shows the starboard aft corner, with two bunks and lockers. The bulkhead door to the galley has six locking handles, called dogs, that were necessary to securely close the door, since this was a watertight bulkhead.

The bunks are arranged four to a side, two upper and two lower, as seen in this view of the forward starboard corner of the crew quarters. The door to the forward compartments is at left and a modern fire extinguisher is secured to the support member.

The interior surfaces of the ELCO 80-foot PT boat galleys were painted in a fire-retardant white paint. High-wear surfaces, like those in passageways and on the cabinets seen here, could be painted in white enamel. (PT Boats, Inc.)

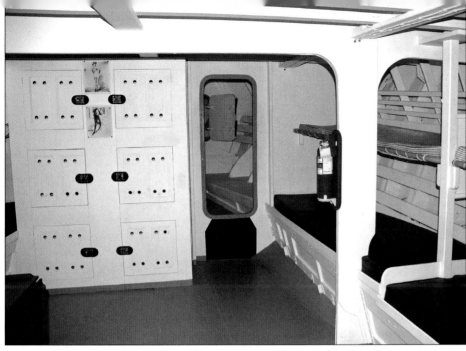

A unit with six lockers (and WWII-vintage pinups) is at the center of the forward bulkhead in this view looking from the rear to the forward end of the crew quarters.

The crew's lockers are made of western red cedar with mahogany door frames. Note the bright latches and the ventilating holes in the doors. The forward port bunks are to the left.

Battened storage bins were provided on the inner hull, outboard of the upper bunks. They were screwed to the diagonal beam braces.

The galley can be glimpsed through the open hatch in this view of the aft bulkhead from the forward side of the crew quarters. A bench is built into the center of the bulkhead and there is a drop-leaf table in the foreground.

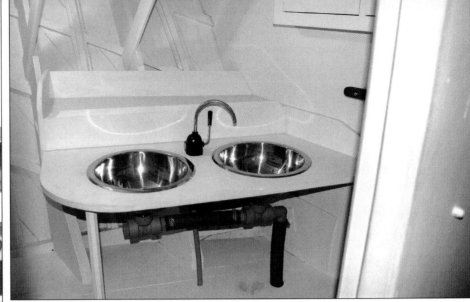

The crew's head, or lavatory, is forward of the crew's quarters, below the foredeck. The twin sinks are on the port side of the hull; the originally issued sinks and counters were stainless steel. A medicine cabinet is on the aft bulkhead.

To the starboard side of the crew's head is a passageway, with the small hatch to the forepeak (seen opened at the left). This photo gives a good view of the network of transverse, longitudinal, and diagonal frames of the boat. Also visible are the steep diagonal joints of the inner layer of hull planking.

There are cushions on the built-in bench on the bulkhead in this World War II photo of the crew quarters. The builder's specifications for this series of boats called for a folding, mahogany-top table mounted on tubular stanchions, with provisions to bolt it to the inboard girder. The table was to have two drop leaves and one drawer. The table top was to have rounded corners and raised edges all around. (PT Boats, Inc.)

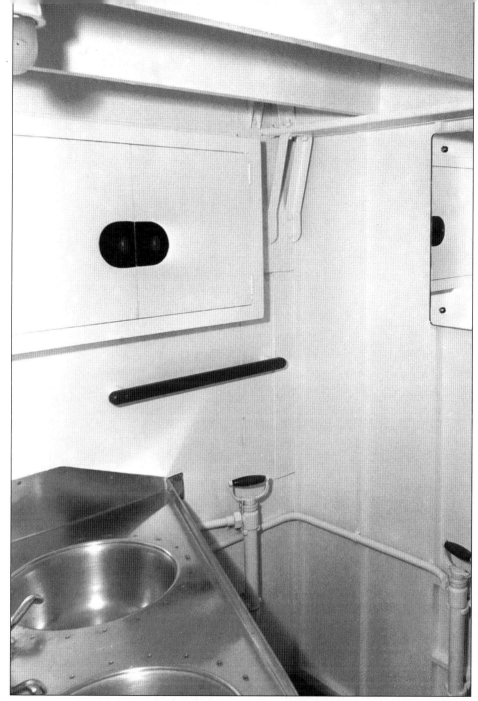

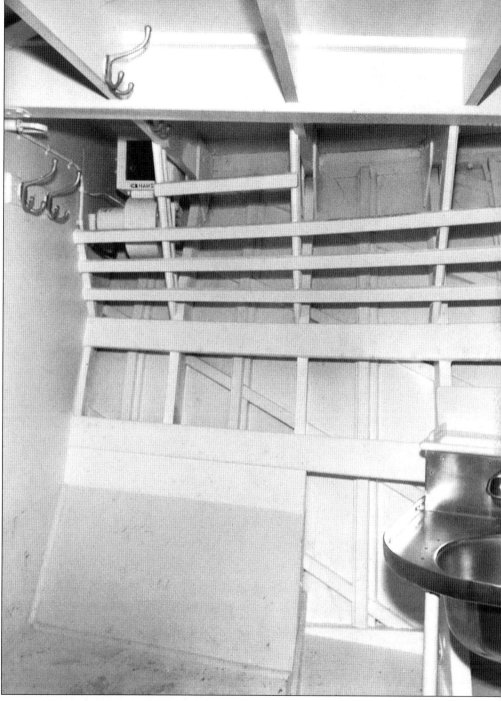

The sink and counter, forward bulkhead with medicine cabinet, and hand pumps for sink water appear in this wartime photo of the crew's head. A grab rail is attached to the bulkhead below the medicine cabinet. To the right is a mirror. (PT Boats, Inc.)

At the aft outboard corner of the crew's head is a ventilator (upper left). Coat hooks were provided in this area. At the bottom left is a built-in drip tray, lined with canvas oil cloth. (PT Boats, Inc.)

The toilet in the aft part of the crew's head is operated by a hand pump on the side. To the left is the curtain in the entry door in the fore-aft partition. On the wall are grab rails, a medicine cabinet (with plumbing diagram thumb-tacked to the door), and a toilet paper holder. (PT Boats, Inc.)

The toilet in the crew's head aboard PT 617 has been rotated as compared with the toilet that appears in the wartime photograph to the left. On PT 617, the hinges for the toilet seat are turned toward the aft bulkhead rather than toward the fore-aft partition. Grab rails and the toilet paper holder are also missing.

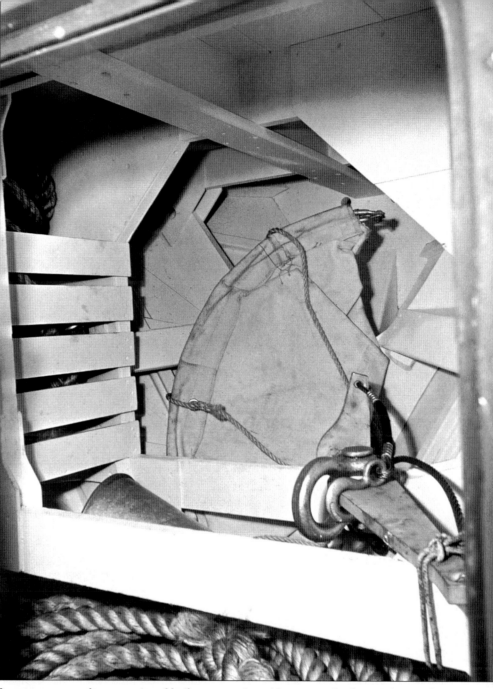

At the forward end of the passageway to the starboard of the head is the crash bulkhead with a small, watertight hatch leading into the forepeak. Stored on chocks to the starboard side of the hatch in this WWII photograph is a spare Danforth anchor and lashings. (PT Boats, Inc.)

A canvas sea anchor was stored in the compartment known as the forepeak, seen here from the passageway adjacent to the crew's head. To the left is a storage bin formed from hardwood battens to hold rope and chain for the anchor. To the far right is part of the watertight rubber gasket around the hatch opening. (PT Boats, Inc.)

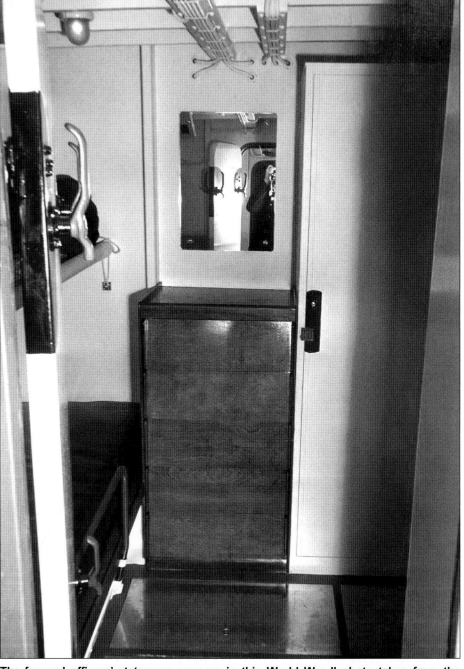

The forward officers' stateroom (also called the petty officers' cabin or stateroom) is to the port of the centerline of the boat, with the galley adjacent to it on the starboard side of the boat. In this photo, the door to the galley is to the far right, with a bookshelf attached to the fore-aft partition. In the corner is a built-in desk with a 20-inch x 27-inch lift top with an exposed piano hinge.

The forward officers' stateroom appears in this World War II photo taken from the officers' head. On the left are the lower, transom berth and upper, boat-style berth. To the right of the berths are a dresser with a mirror over it and a locker. Flooring was balsa-core aluminum-covered panels with mahogany spacers, removable to allow access to the bilges. (PT Boats, Inc.)

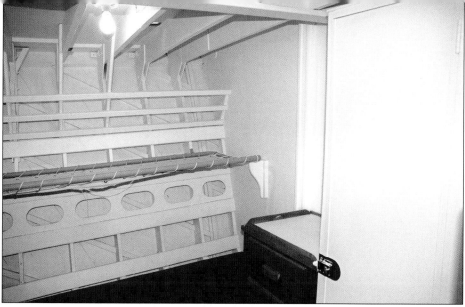

On the starboard side of the forward officers' stateroom are a transom berth (at bottom) and locker (to the far right). As in many living spaces within the hull, battens are fastened to the deck braces to form storage bins.

While there were provisions on late-war ELCO 80-foot PT boats for an upper, boat-type berth in the forward officers' stateroom, these berths were rarely used.

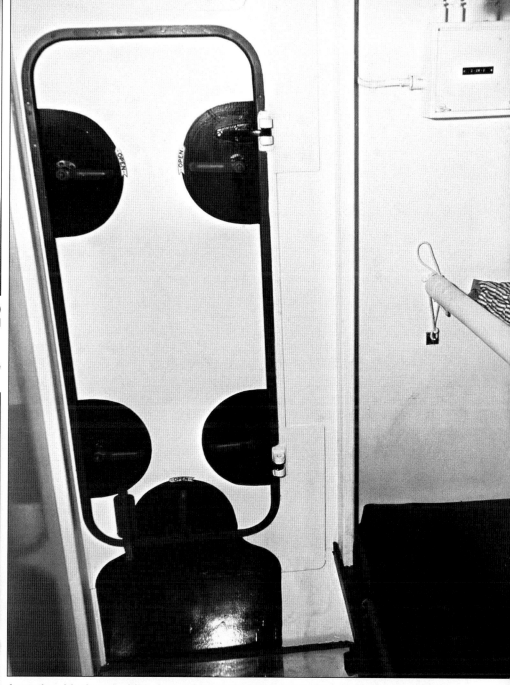

A wartime black-and-white photo shows the watertight bulkhead on the aft side of the forward officers' stateroom. The watertight doors were made of aluminum and plywood and had quick-operating dogs, special hinges, and rubber gaskets fitted around the openings.(PT Boats, Inc.)

A WWII-era view of the aft inboard corner of the forward officers' stateroom shows the aft locker to the right, the door to the galley at center, and the desk, bookshelf, and fan to the left. (PT Boats, Inc.)

The sink in the officers' head differs from those in the crew's head. The aft outboard corner of the officers' head, seen here, is immediately aft of the forward officers' stateroom. To the left is the door into the aft officers' stateroom.

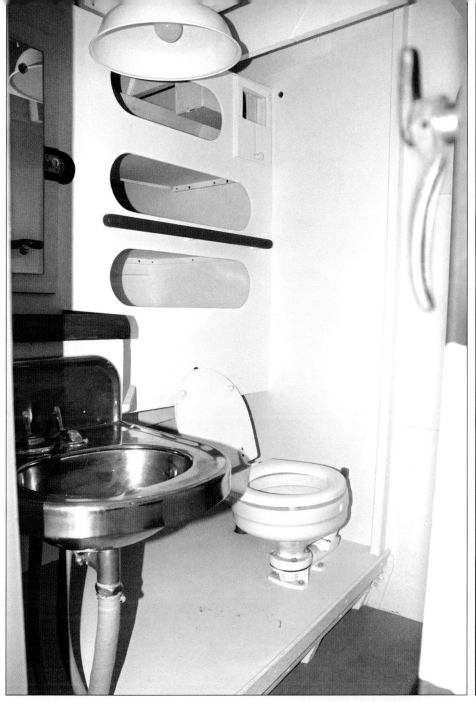

Above the toilet, which is next to the sink, are three inset towel shelves, which like the bulk of the boat are made from wood. A simple, utilitarian light fixture hangs from the ceiling. This type of light fixture was widely used inside the PT boats.

The toilet hand pump is next to the toilet bowl in this WWII-era photo of the officers' head. Holders for toilet paper and paper towels are attached to the bulkhead next to the toilet. To the right is the closed and secured watertight door. (PT Boats, Inc.)

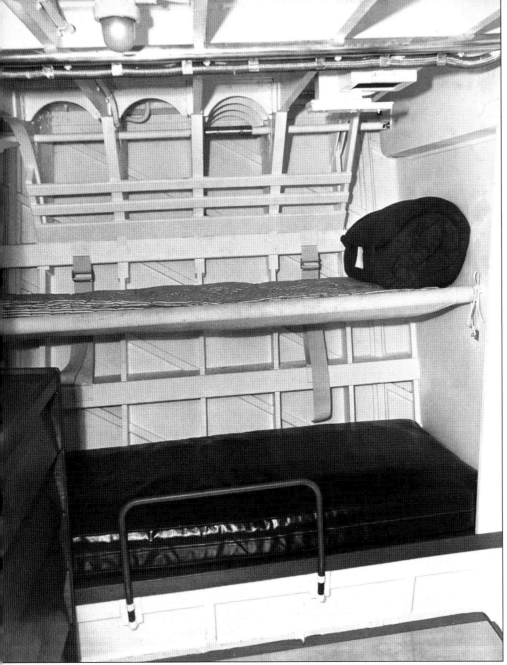

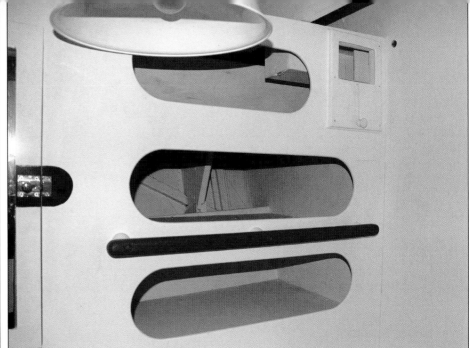

Towel shelves and a grab bar that doubled as a towel bar are located above the toilet in the officers' head. To the right of the upper shelf is a vent, with a sliding door to regulate the draft.

The fore-aft partition in the officers' head has a grab rail. To the right is the open watertight door to the rear officers' stateroom.

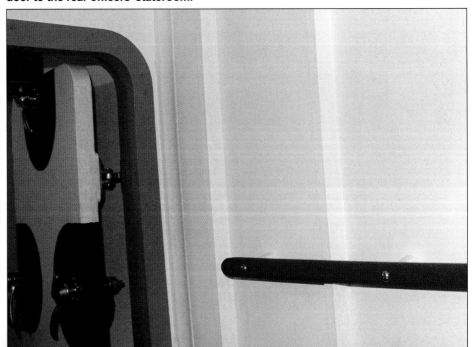

The very cramped aft officers' stateroom was sometimes called the commanding officer's stateroom or cabin. This vintage black-and-white photo shows the ceiling light, electrical conduits, and batten storage bin on the hull next to the upper berth, as well as the mattresses on the berths and the vent outlet above the bed (upper right of photo) in the room. (PT Boats, Inc.)

In this photo of the aft officers' stateroom (sometimes referred to as the commanding officer's cabin) on PT 617, a bureau (lower left) is in the aft part of the compartment, with a transom berth (lower) and boat-type berth along the hull wall.

On the lower berth is a life vest, while on the upper berth are a lantern and a sea chest with the insignia of Motor Torpedo Boat Squadron (MTB RON) 35.

Lockers are at left and a bureau at right in this black-and-white archival photo of the aft officers' stateroom. Above the bureau is a case with a glazed door; inside it is a key rack and electrical lines. (PT Boats, Inc.)

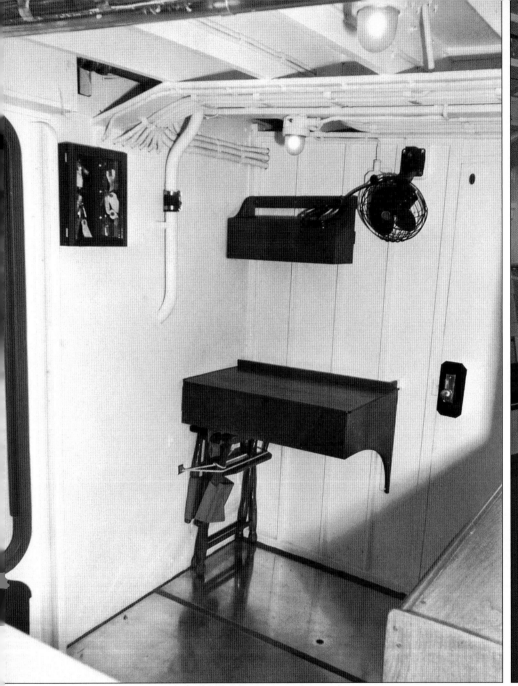

Mounted to the fore-aft partition in the aft officers' stateroom is a 30-inch-wide desk, with a folding chair secured to the bulkhead below it. The door to the officers' head is to the left. There is a key case to the right of the doorway. Floor panels are aluminum with mahogany dividers, as originally installed on the ELCO 80-foot boats. (PT Boats, Inc.)

There are weapon racks on the fore-aft partition outside of the aft officers' stateroom, which is visible through the door to the left. The lower racks held rifles. Above the rifle racks are cutlass racks. There was some variation in this area between individual boats, which was the case for the radio area as well.

The cutlass racks as viewed from forward. The ladder at extreme right goes to the chart house and bridge.

The rifle rack was designed to hold four weapons for crew members. Rifle butts fit into the routed area on the lower shelf while the rifle barrels slid into upper-shelf notches..

The wardroom is located across the centerline of the hull from the aft officers' stateroom. It was also called the officers' mess, and some plans identify the compartment as the armory. A mahogany plywood mess table was installed next to the starboard side of the hull

Two bench seats with cushions face each other at the fore and aft sides of the table.

A space called the radar room is actually part of the wardroom. Forward of the table and forward seat, on the forward bulkhead, are two electrical boxes. There is also a radar unit with scope at the lower center of the photo.

The radar unit rests on brackets on of the floor. Electrical wiring associated with the radar is not installed.

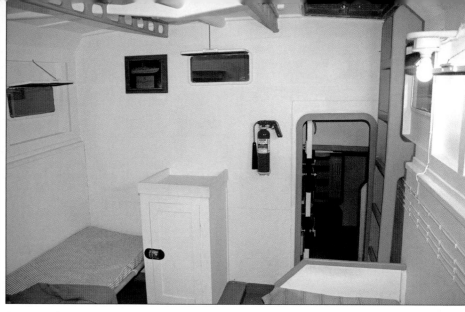

Under the windows along the starboard side of the day cabin (or dayroom) is a berth. The blackout shades on the side windows are in the raised position. The forward shade is bifolding, to accommodate the ladder fixed in front of the window. Visible at the lower left is the door forward into the wardroom, where there are a table and seat.

At the aft end of the day cabin are crew lockers, a medicine cabinet, and shelves. The door with the five dogs to the left of center leads to the engine room. Above that door is a door with an outlet on the after deck; this door was designed to be wide enough to allow a patient on a stretcher to be passed through it. Aft of the sea chest at the upper right is part of the after turret that protrudes into the day cabin; toward the top is a small access door.

The gray frames on the day cabin ceiling are roof stiffeners, with cutouts so they could also act as handrails. Berths with water-repellent cushions lined both sides of the cabin; unlike the built-in berths shown here, they were of roll-up canvas construction with removable tubular metal headrails. The floor and furnishings were designed to be easily removable, to allow access to the fuel tanks located below the day cabin.

The tubular head rails of the berths can be seen in this wartime image of the aft end of the day cabin. As originally specified for the series of ELCO 80-foot PT boats to which PT 617 belonged, the door to the engine room was to have a double-pane glass window, as shown at the top of the door in this photo. Webbing straps secured the roll-up berths when stored. On the aft bulkhead was a fire extinguisher. (PT Boats, Inc.)

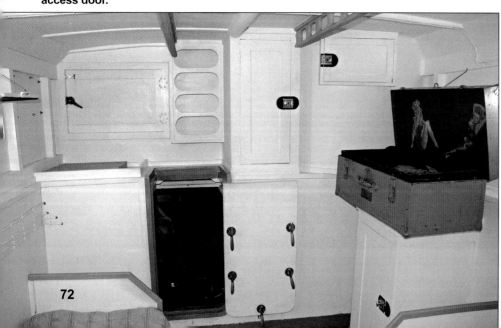

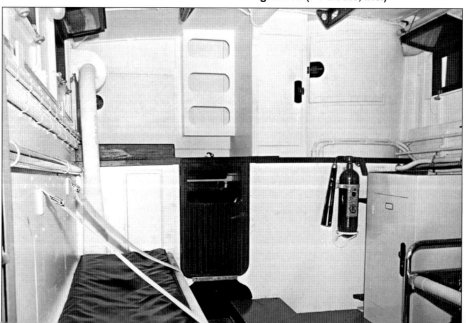

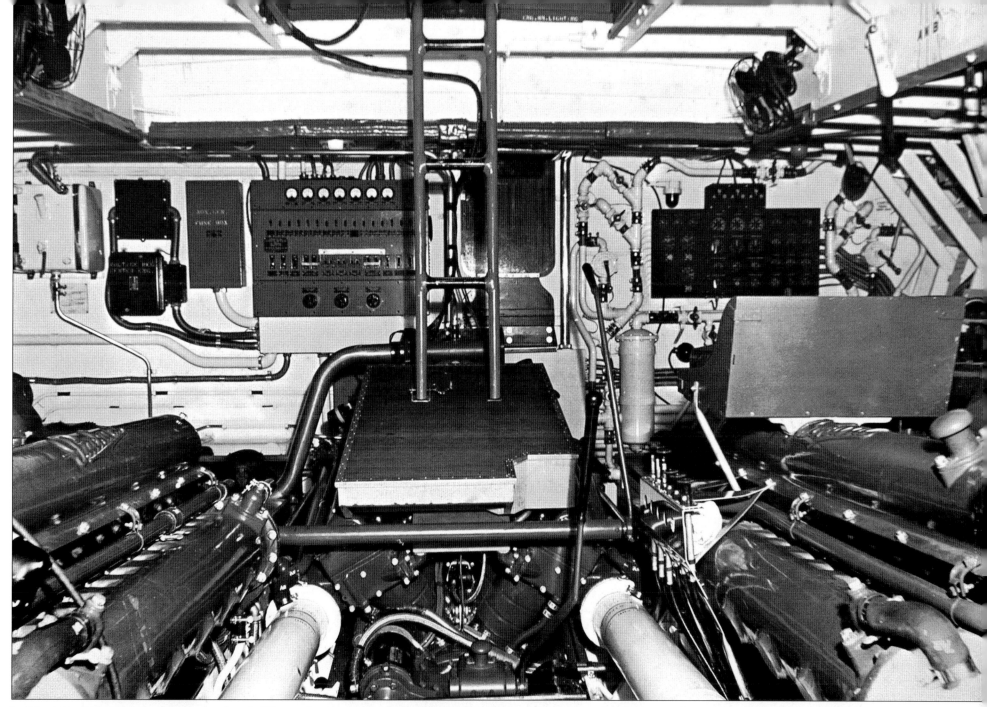

In this vintage photograph of the forward end of the engine room of an ELCO 80-foot PT boat, the ladder above the platform at the center leads up to the engine room hatchway. The small door beyond the ladder leads to the day cabin. To the right of the door are the instrument panel and a forward-facing seat, and to the left of the door are the electrical panel, fuse boxes, and voltage regulator. Below are the three Packard V-12 4M-2500 water-cooled engines. (PT Boats, Inc.)

Two sailors perform work on the port engine of an ELCO 80-foot PT boat on which the engine room cover has been removed. The light-colored pipes are engine exhausts that exit the aft side of the compartment, at top. The worker at left is facing the aft end of the center engine. In 1944, various basic configurations of the engine locations had been authorized: with the engines abreast at the forward end of the engine compartment, or with the center engine staggered toward the forward end of the engine compartment and the outboard engines to the aft, along with further variations in the drive-train configurations. (PT Boats, Inc.)

At the center of this photo, looking aft at the starboard engine, are the operator's seat and shift levers. The light-colored exhaust lines exit the rear bulkhead of the engine compartment and enter the lazarette, or aft compartment. The small hatch into the lazarette is visible to the far right. (PT Boats, Inc.)

To the lower left in this builder's photo of the forward starboard part of the engine room is the platform over the center engine, with the ladder to the engine room hatchway removed. To the far right is the forward edge of the wooden seat mounted on the forward end of the starboard engine, where a crewman sat when operating the three reverse-gear shifting levers. To the left of the gear shifters is an automatic voltage regulator and one of the two auxiliary generator sets, comprised of a gasoline engine driving a 5.5 kw, 28 1/2 volt DC generator. (PT Boats, Inc.)

A crewman is shown operating the reverse gear-shift levers. The crewman, normally a machinist's mate, would shift the gears following orders from the bridge, when maneuvering at slow speeds, such as while docking or coming athwart of a tender. The crewman's seat is positioned over the center engine – a noisy environment indeed. (PT Boats, Inc.)

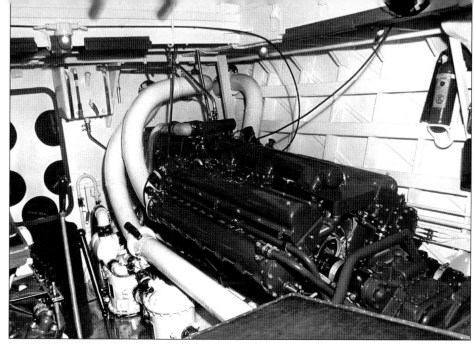

The port engine appears in this picture looking aft. To the far left is the closed hatch to the lazarette. There is a fire extinguisher in the upper right. (PT Boats, Inc.)

Three Packard 4M-2500 engines powered each ELCO 80-foot PT boat. The engine featured a gear-driven centrifugal supercharger. The starter was electric, and the generator was rated at 28 volts, 40 amps. Depending upon the number of engines used and the rates of speed and rpm, the engines could consume anywhere from 17-1/2 to 474 gallons of fuel per hour.

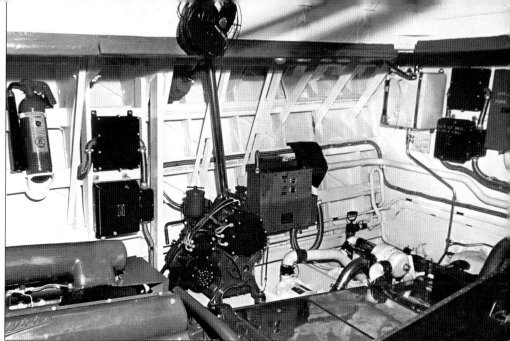

The forward port corner of the engine compartment is viewed here from the starboard side of the room. Below the ventilation fan is the port auxiliary generator set, with an exhaust tube leading up from it. At the bottom left of the picture is the forward end of the port engine. (PT Boats, Inc.)

Another view of the forward port corner of the engine compartment. The Packard engines were cooled by sea water that was routed through an elaborate plumbing network. (PT Boats, Inc.)

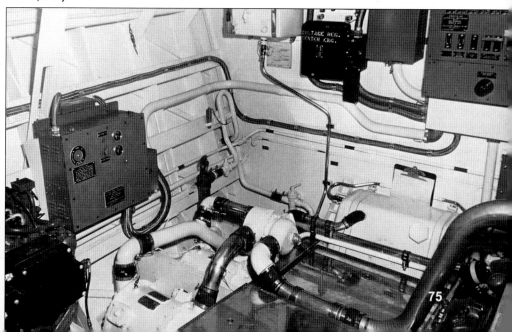

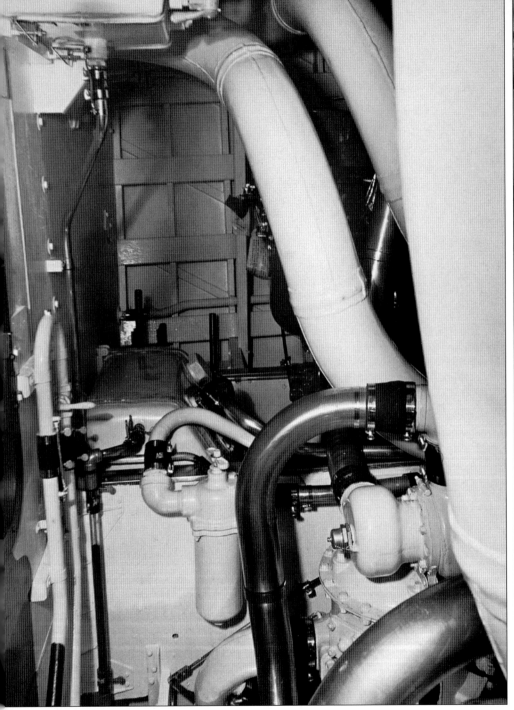

The port engine exhausts enter the lazarette bulkhead as seen in this view of the port aft corner of the engine room. (PT Boats, Inc.)

The opened hatch into the lazarette is at the extreme right in this view of the space aft of the starboard engine. (PT Boats, Inc.)

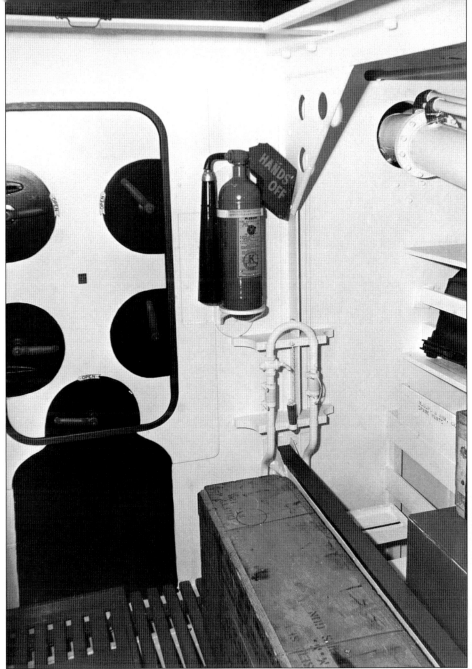

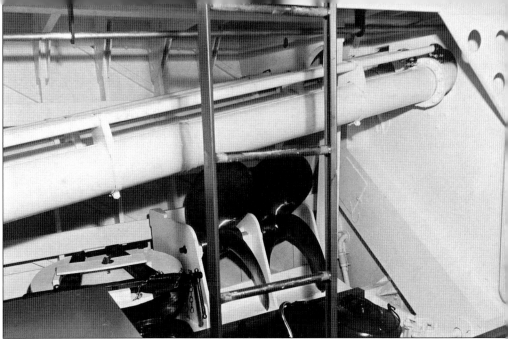

This view of the forward port corner of the lazarette shows the three port exhaust lines that cross the compartment from fore to aft. The metal ladder in front of the exhaust pipes leads up to the hatch on the afterdeck near the stern. Various items are stored under the exhaust pipes, including two spare propellers on a bracket. (PT Boats, Inc.)

At the center of the transom between the exhaust lines inside the lazarette is a workbench with vise and a drawer. The rod suspended from strapping near the top of the photo is the operating rod for the butterfly valves on the starboard exhaust outlets. There was a similar rod on the port side of the lazarette. (PT Boats, Inc.)

The watertight bulkhead and hatch between the lazarette and the engine room are seen here from within the lazarette. A Kidde fire extinguisher with a "Hands Off" stenciling on the lever guard hangs to the starboard of the hatch. Spare parts boxes and ammunition were also stored in this compartment. The lazarette's flooring consisted of removable sections of slats. (PT Boats, Inc.)

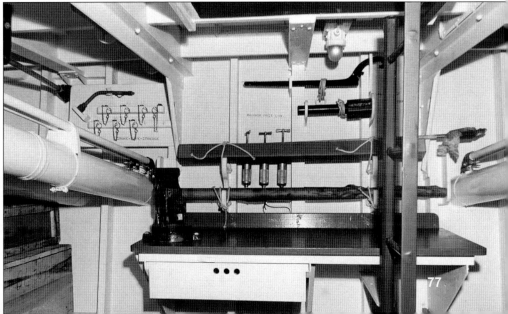

Weapon Positions

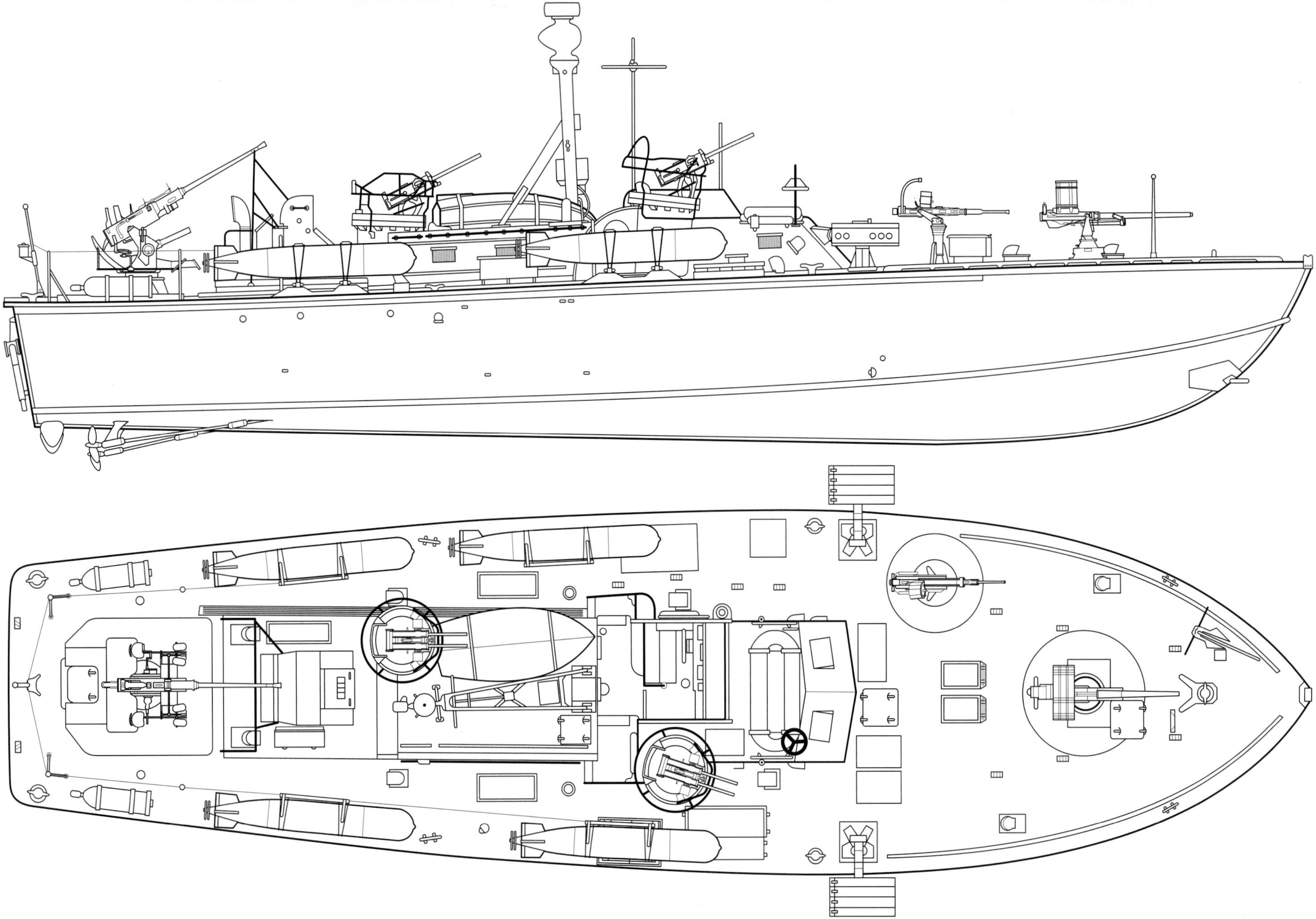

Deck Guns

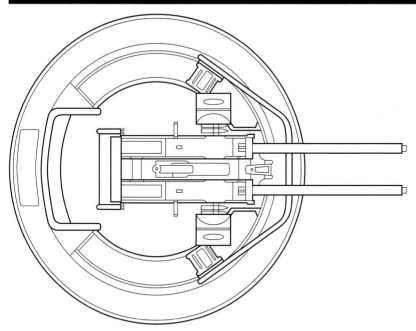

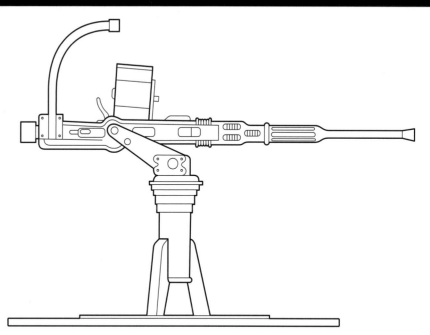

Twin belt-fed, air cooled, .50 cal. Browning M2 Machine Guns: 550 rounds per minute (rpm), muzzle velocity of 2930 feet per second (fps), maximum effective range 2500 yards, maximum range 4.2 miles, 710 grain FMJ bullet, powder charge 235 grains.

Each boat featured two Browning M2 Machine Gun positions.

M4 20mm Oerlikon cannon: 60 round capacity magazine, 480 rpm, muzzle velocity 2740 fps, range 5500 yards, 8.5 oz round weight.

37 mm Oldsmobile M9 cannon; 30 round magazine, 125 rpm, muzzle velocity 2000 fps, range 8875 yards.

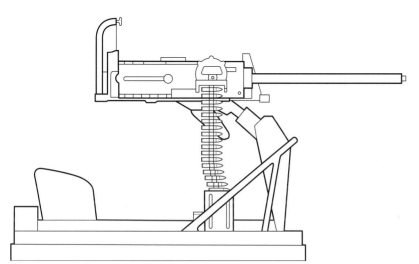

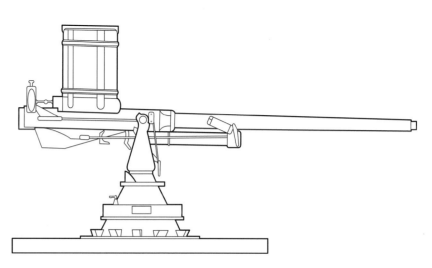

Introduced in July 1944, Measure 31, Design 5P utilized Navy Green (5-NG) and Ocean Green (5-OG). It was hoped that this type of pattern could mask the boat's speed and course when observed from shore or other ships, but it was later determined that such schemes increased the visibility of the boats to Kamikazes.

This is the paint scheme that John F. Kennedy's famed PT109 wore when it was delivered by ELCO. There is some evidence, however, that by the time Kennedy took command the boat was painted in a color known at Motor Torpedo Boat green.